THE HERITAGE COLLECTION

Empress Eléni
Itege of Ethiopia

Letitia deGraft Okyere

Illustrated by Masum Ahmed

Empress Eléni: Itege of Ethiopia

Copyright © 2024 by Letitia deGraft Okyere

Illustrator: Masum Ahmed

Layout designer: Nasim Malik Sarkar

Library of Congress Control Number: 2024911478

All rights reserved.

No part of this publication may be reproduced, stored in a retrieval system, a database, and/or published in any form or by any means, electronic, mechanical, photocopying, recording or otherwise, without the prior written permission of the publisher.

ISBN 978-1-956776-24-9 hardback
ISBN 978-1-956776-25-6 epub

Published by Lion's Historian Press
https://www.lionshistorian.net/

For

Sarah, Abigail, and Hadassah

A Brief Introduction

The Kingdom of Ethiopia, formerly Abyssinia, was founded by kings or emperors belonging to the Solomonic Dynasty. They claimed direct descent from King Solomon of ancient Israel and his relationship with Makeda, Queen of Sheba. The first emperor, Yekuno Amlak, ruled from 1270 to 1285 under the regnal name Tasfa Iyasus.

Emperor Amda Seyon, believed by some to be the grandson of Yekuno Amlak, reigned from 1314 to 1344. Amda Seyon expanded Ethiopia's territories to include neighboring Muslim kingdoms or sultanates such as Hadiya. Hadiya and other vassals were allowed to maintain a great deal of their independence but paid annual tribute to Ethiopia. In the later years of his reign, Emperor Amda Seyon demanded that Amano, Sultan of Hadiya, show respect to his overlord; Amano refused. Amda Seyon attacked Hadiya and reminded the kingdom that it had been conquered by Ethiopia.

Over time, Hadiya rebuilt its army, which was estimated to include 40,000 horsemen and 80,000 foot soldiers. Its people learned advanced agricultural methods, growing different kinds of grains. The local currency was pieces of iron. Hadiya's merchants depended on the port of Zeila in present-day Somalia for trade with the Near East, like Persia (now Iran) and India.

Contents

Chapter 1:   A Daughter of Hadiya 1
Chapter 2:   Ethiopia Invades Hadiya 3
Chapter 3:   Empress Eléni 5
Chapter 4:   Eléni the Author 7
Chapter 5:   Queen Mother Eléni 9
Chapter 6:   Guardian of the Royal Household 11
Chapter 7:   An Influential Courtier 13
Chapter 8:   Ethiopia's Regent 15
Chapter 9:   An Ethiopian Diplomat 17
Chapter 10:   Eléni's Regency Ends 19
Chapter 11:   Eléni Retires to Gojjam 21
Epilogue: The Dowager Empress Eléni 23

A Short Note 25
Glossary 27
Quiz 29
Word Search Puzzle 31
Timeline 33
Family Tree 34
References 35
Fun Fact About Ethiopia 37
Other Books in the Heritage Collection 38
Author's Note 41

Chapter - 1

A Daughter of Hadiya

Many centuries ago, a little princess lived in the Kingdom of Hadiya. Though no one knows her birth name, she became Eléni of Ethiopia. Eléni was sometimes referred to as the queen of Zeila because Muslim states in the Horn of Africa were collectively known as Zeila, named after the large port city of Zeila in what is now Somalia. It is believed that Eléni was born in the 1430s, when Hadiya was Ethiopia's subject. Eléni's father was the Garad or sultan of Hadiya called Mahmad.

Eléni was an intelligent child who enjoyed reading and writing. She studied ancient Muslim scripts and watched her father at work, where she learned to bargain in government matters. Eléni's father encouraged her to build communication skills through exchanges at his court. Garad Mahmad recognized he had a gifted daughter who would be a great asset to Hadiya. She might even help to remove Ethiopia as its overlord one day.

During her break from studies, Eléni took walks or horse rides in the palace gardens. Often, Eléni went beyond the palace gates on horseback, through Hadiya's fertile fields used for growing grains. When Eléni met farmers along the way, she stopped to ask about their well-being.

Chapter - 2

Ethiopia Invades Hadiya

Eléni was young when Garad Mahmad died, and her brother Mahiko became the new Garad. Eléni's father had objected to Hadiya's vassal status but remained obedient. Garad Mahiko, on the other hand, was rebellious, and Eléni worried that his attitude would lead to unrest.

Emperor Zara Yaqob demanded Mahiko's presence at his court, asking for Ethiopia's tribute. In years past, after Ethiopia's Emperor Amda Seyon conquered Hadiya, payment of its yearly tribute kept the peace. Eléni pleaded with her brother, advising him to pay Hadiya's tribute to Ethiopia. She reminded Mahiko of Hadiya's destruction when an old leader, Amano, refused to make payment. Mahiko ignored Eléni's warning and sent a refusal to Emperor Yaqob.

Around 1444, Emperor Yaqob invaded Hadiya. He captured Eléni and decided to marry her. Eléni agreed, hoping the marriage would end Ethiopia's attack on Hadiya and save Mahiko. Sadly, Eléni's future marriage to Emperor Yaqob did not help Mahiko. Eléni's brother died during the conflict he caused. Nonetheless, Eléni kept to the bargain and moved to Ethiopia.

Chapter - 3

Empress Eléni

In 1445, Eléni, married Emperor Zara Yaqob. He gave her the honored title *Itege*. Later, when she was baptized as a Christian in the Ethiopian Church, her name changed to Eléni, meaning "light," a form of Helen. After her coronation as Emperor Yaqob's wife, she became Empress Eléni.

At the royal court, Empress Eléni gained an understanding of Ethiopian affairs and social change. Eléni read books on law and politics, allowing her to shape royal court decisions. She gave Emperor Yaqob sound advice, leading to his defeat of his enemies. Eléni helped Emperor Yaqob to establish a new capital city and rearrange the army. Through Eléni's influence, Emperor Yaqob allowed Ethiopia's Muslim territories a degree of freedom. He appointed governors rather than join these lands to Ethiopia.

Empress Eléni was kind to the people, donating money to the poor. She was a gifted cook, preparing delicious meals for the royal table. Eléni pleased Emperor Yaqob so much that he made her senior queen, above his other two wives. Historians write that Emperor Yaqob was one of Ethiopia's greatest rulers. No doubt, this is because he had Empress Eléni at his side.

Chapter - 4

Eléni the Author

Eléni embraced her new destiny as a Christian, even though she grew up practicing Islam. She studied theology and became familiar with the Ethiopian Church. Eléni added to Ethiopian literature by writing two books on Christianity. One of her books was a study of the Trinity and life of St. Mary. Eléni's other book studied the laws of God and how these laws affected daily living.

When Eléni sat at Emperor Zara Yaqob's court, she heard about disagreements within the Ethiopian Church. Eléni thought many of these problems occurred because the Ethiopian Church did not have enough religious writings in *Geez*, its language. Eléni arranged to have experts translate many religious Greek and Arabic writings into Geez. These texts helped to resolve some of the issues that divided the Ethiopian Church.

Chapter - 5

Queen Mother Eléni

In 1468, Empress Eléni's husband died, and he was succeeded by his son, Baeda Maryam I. Baeda Maryam I was born after his father married Empress Eléni and had a close bond with her, especially after his mother died. He loved Eléni and considered her to be his mother.

The new emperor remembered Empress Eléni's valuable contributions in the past. Baeda Maryam I honored Eléni with the title given to an emperor's favorite wife. Her new role became that of queen mother. Queen Mother Eléni assisted Baeda Maryam I with political affairs. She encouraged him to keep governments of Ethiopia's conquests small and allow control by local families. Eléni designed churches ordered by Emperor Baeda Maryam I.

Queen Mother Eléni wanted peace between Ethiopia and neighboring Adal because it would improve trade in the region. Adal and Ethiopia had a history of going to battle and Adal had been defeated by Emperor Zara Yaqob in the last one. So, when Baeda Maryam I became emperor, Adal asked for a peace treaty. Eléni helped restore harmony with Adal. Later, the peace deal failed, forcing Ethiopia into battle again. Emperor Maryam I depended on Eléni's wise counsel.

Chapter - 6

Guardian of the Royal Household

The respected and wise Queen Mother Eléni remained at the palace when Baeda Maryam I died after ten years. Emperor Eskender succeeded his father, reigning from 1478-1494. Eléni helped Emperor Eskender administer affairs of state, just as she had with Baeda Maryam I. As Ethiopia had to continue its battle with the neighboring Adal Kingdom, Emperor Eskender leaned on Eléni's experience.

Queen Mother Eléni was so powerful at the royal court that a nobleman called Mikael desired to have Eléni removed. The nobleman did not like Eléni's close relationship with Emperor Eskender and he devised a wicked plan against Eléni. Eléni uncovered the plot against her, and the nobleman was forced to leave the palace. Eléni kept her role as government adviser at the palace and this pleased Emperor Eskender.

Chapter - 7

An Influential Courtier

Eléni remained at the palace after Emperor Eskender's death at twenty-two years. Emperor Eskender's brother Naod became emperor after a succession dispute, and he ruled from 1494 to 1508. Emperor Naod trusted Eléni to help with running Ethiopia because there were many internal conflicts due to Naod's struggle to become emperor.

Also, when there were external problems, Emperor Naod relied on Eléni's expertise. As a result, Naod won many battles against the Muslim forces. Another peace agreement was offered by Ethiopia's Muslim neighbors, and Eléni advised Emperor Naod to accept it. Eléni tried to ensure that the peace agreement succeeded through intermarriages and negotiations, but it was difficult as each country wanted to rule over the other.

Wise Eléni then advised Emperor Naod to build a relationship with Portugal for trade and help in time of war. At the time, Portugal had discovered a trading passage to India through the Cape of Good Hope in southern Africa. Emperor Naod followed Eléni's directions and sent emissaries from his Ethiopian court to Portugal, offering friendship.

Chapter - 8

Ethiopia's Regent

Eléni appointed Emperor Naod's son to the throne after he died during a war with Adal. The new emperor, Lebna Dengel or Daawit II, was twelve years old. As a result, Eléni became head of the council of regents appointed to rule until Lebna Dengel could lead his kingdom.

During this time, Eléni had churches built or repaired. The Martula Maryam Cathedral in the Gojjam province in northern Ethiopia was one example. Eléni had adopted Gojjam as her home province. This magnificent cathedral was built with wood and stone and had two altars made from gold. A historian wrote that there was so much gold that the Martula Maryam had its own security guards. In addition, Eléni donated funds to the cathedral's monastery to help the priests.

Most importantly, Regent Eléni helped to maintain peace between Ethiopia and Adal. However, Eléni had a vision of Ethiopia's future problems because she knew that Adal was strengthening its armies and building a bond with the growing Ottoman Empire.

Chapter - 9

An Ethiopian Diplomat

Regent Eléni knew that when the peace agreement with Adal failed, Ethiopia would need help fighting its Muslim neighbor. Thus, Eléni desired a relationship with Christian Europe and was pleased when in 1508, Portuguese messengers arrived at the Ethiopian court. The King of Portugal had received the message sent during Emperor Naod's reign.

The ambassadors from Dom Manuel, King of Portugal, were welcomed by Eléni. Naod had died, and Eléni ruled as regent. Eléni worried about Ethiopia being the only Christian state in a region of Muslim states, while Portugal's fort on Socotra Island, in the Indian Ocean, faced threats from Egypt's fleet. The King of Portugal also wanted a friendship with Ethiopia.

In response, Eléni sent an ambassador called Mateus to the King of Portugal with gifts and a letter. Eléni's letter, written in 1509, promised to stand with Portugal against Portugal's enemies. Eléni believed that a union of the Ethiopian army and Portugal's navy would make a strong force. Mateus' journey was full of problems, but he made it to Portugal in 1514. In 1517, Mateus commenced his journey back to Ethiopia with King Manuel's ambassador, Rodrigo da Lima. The Portuguese king promised to help Ethiopia fight warriors from Adal.

Chapter - 10

Eléni's Regency Ends

Eléni's regency ended when Emperor Lebna Dengle became an adult and took over the empire. It was at this time, in 1520, that the second Portuguese emissaries arrived in Ethiopia. Emperor Lebna Dengle did not have the same understanding of Ethiopia's problems as Eléni. As a result, Portugal's ambassador, Rodrigo da Lima, did not have a role to play.

Eléni had asked Lebna Dengle to build strength through an alliance with Portugal before going to war. Emperor Lebna Dengle had ignored Eléni's advice and gone to war against Adal. So, when the Portuguese emissaries arrived in Ethiopia, Lebna Dengle had grown confident. He believed he did not need Portugal's assistance because he had defeated Adal with only Ethiopian forces. Later, Lebna Dengle was defeated, and he saw Eléni's wisdom in building alliances with Europe.

Even though Eléni disagreed with Emperor Lebna Dengle regarding going to war with Adal, Emperor Lebna Dengle had respect for Eléni. Many courtiers wished Eléni would remain at the palace because she taught Emperor Lebna Dengle to rule with compassion.

Chapter - 11

Eléni Retires to Gojjam

Eléni retired to her estates in the Gojjam district during Emperor Lebna Dengle's reign. However, the Dowager Empress Eléni attended events at the emperor's court, though she was in her eighties. She was seen with Emperor Lebna Dengle's mother, Naod Mogasa, and his wife, Sabla Wangel. Eléni participated in the service where the late Emperor Naod's remains were blessed and reburied. She continued to support the monastery at the Martula Maryam Cathedral and helping the poor. Eléni's influence in Gojjam increased.

An aged Eléni died in 1522, and Emperor Lebna Dengle buried her at the Martula Maryam Cathedral. Empress Eléni's subjects mourned her death. They believed they had died, too, because when Eléni lived, she had defended and protected them. Months and months after Empress Eléni's death, many still went to the emperor's court to mourn her loss because of the love and respect they had for her.

Epilogue

The Dowager Empress Eléni

Eléni, a princess of Hadiya, grew to become an Itege of Ethiopia. Empress Eléni provided strong leadership and diplomacy skills, guiding the reign of five emperors across three generations. Empress Eléni negotiated peace deals, donated money to the poor, had churches built, and helped to resolve theological questions. In addition, Empress Eléni challenged the political and social practices of the time and demonstrated a woman's capacity to direct national affairs.

Today, many acknowledge Empress Eléni's significant impact on Ethiopia, and her name remains revered across the world. The Nigist Eléni Mohammed Memorial Hospital in Hosaina, a southern Ethiopian town, is named after Empress Eléni.

A Short Note

Some accounts of Eléni's life point to Baeda Maryam I as her husband. Primary sources of information for historians are the chronicles of Zara Yaqob and Baeda Maryam I, believed to have been written when Lebna Dengle was emperor. A French researcher translated and published the chronicles in 1893.

These records refer to Eléni as Ite Zan Zela, right-hand empress of Zara Yaqob, and the sister of Mahiko, Garad of Hadiya. Reputable historians have confirmed this version of events. On the other hand, the chronicles of some later emperors note that Eléni was the wife of Baeda Maryam I. This version is supported by a different set of historians due to assumptions made from the chronicles of Zara Yaqob and Baeda Maryam I. To date, both viewpoints remain as writers continue the debate.

It is important to note that regardless of which emperor married Eléni, her role in the courts of several Ethiopian emperors is not in dispute. Empress Eléni is accepted as a woman who brought about political and cultural change in Ethiopia, setting the pace for empresses like Taytu Betul, who came after her.

Glossary

Hadiya	The Hadiya Sultanate was an ancient kingdom in Africa.
Garad	A term used to describe a governor or leader in an Islamic kingdom.
Ethiopia	A country in the eastern part of Africa.
Coronation	This is when a crown is put on the head of a man, making him king, or on the head of a woman, making her queen.
Geez	The ancient language used in Ethiopia. In modern times, the Ethiopian Church uses the language.
Adal	The Adal Sultanate was in the eastern part of Africa. Adal was founded during Emperor Amda Seyon's conflict with the Sultanate of Ifat.
Regent	The person who controls a country because the king or queen is too young or not able to rule.
Martula Maryam	The ancient cathedral built by Eléni.
Ottoman Empire	A strong nation that controlled parts of three continents, Europe, Asia, and Africa, from the 1300s to the early 1900s.
Sultanate	A country, state, or kingdom ruled by a sultan. A sultan is a leader with religious importance.

Gojjam	A region in the northeastern part of Ethiopia.
Horn of Africa	A region in East Africa that includes countries such as Ethiopia, Somalia, Eritrea, and Djibouti. It is sometimes extended to include Kenya, South Sudan, Sudan, and Uganda.
Ifat	Ifat was a Muslim state that existed in eastern Africa from about 1300-1500. The kingdom extended to parts of present-day Ethiopia, Somalia, and Djibouti. As Ifat fell, Adal formed to continue the resistance to Ethiopia's advances.
Dowager	Refers to a wealthy widow. Commonly used for widows belonging to aristocratic families.

Quiz

1. When was Eléni born?

    (a) 1430s
    (b) 1450s
    (c) 1550s
    (d) 1560s

2. Where was Eléni's born?

    (a) Adal
    (b) Ethiopia
    (c) Hadiya
    (d) Portugal

3. What was the name of Eléni's brother?

    (a) Mahiko
    (b) Maryam
    (c) Mateus
    (d) Mahmad

4. Who was Eléni's husband?

    (a) Emperor Eskende
    (b) Emperor Lebna Dengle
    (c) Emperor Zara Yaqob
    (d) Emperor Naod

5. With which country did Eléni's want to build a friendship?

   (a) France
   (b) Portugal
   (c) Germany
   (d) Russia

6. Where did Eléni have her retirement estate?

   (a) Adal
   (b) Hadiya
   (c) Sawa
   (d) Gojjam

Quiz Answers: ACACBD

Word Search Puzzle

C	E	S	K	E	N	D	E	R	K	L	M	S	S
B	C	M	S	V	T	R	Y	P	K	N	E	M	U
H	W	H	M	E	N	E	N	L	R	N	B	B	S
Z	M	E	N	E	L	I	K	M	N	M	S	A	E
H	K	Z	Y	A	Q	O	B	A	C	M	H	E	N
S	N	E	X	T	S	T	H	B	X	K	L	D	Y
E	Y	W	B	R	K	O	Z	S	M	Z	N	A	O
B	L	D	Q	M	Y	P	T	A	Y	T	U	G	S
L	M	I	R	V	O	H	B	A	K	A	F	F	A
E	B	T	S	N	T	T	J	Y	N	W	X	T	B
B	Y	U	U	L	Z	S	E	L	A	S	S	I	E
K	N	K	Y	N	B	W	S	P	Z	T	K	R	R
X	E	Y	T	E	W	O	D	R	O	S	R	T	X
Y	M	X	M	T	M	E	N	T	E	W	A	B	Y

Word Search Puzzle Answers:

Emperors and Empresses of Ethiopia's Solomonic Dynasty

1. YEKUNO
2. SUSENYOS
3. MENELIK
4. ZEWDITU
5. SELASSIE
6. YOHANNES
7. MENTEWAB
8. BAKAFFA
9. TEWODROS
10. YAQOB
11. BAEDA
12. TAYTU
13. ESKENDER
14. MENEN
15. SEBLE

Timeline

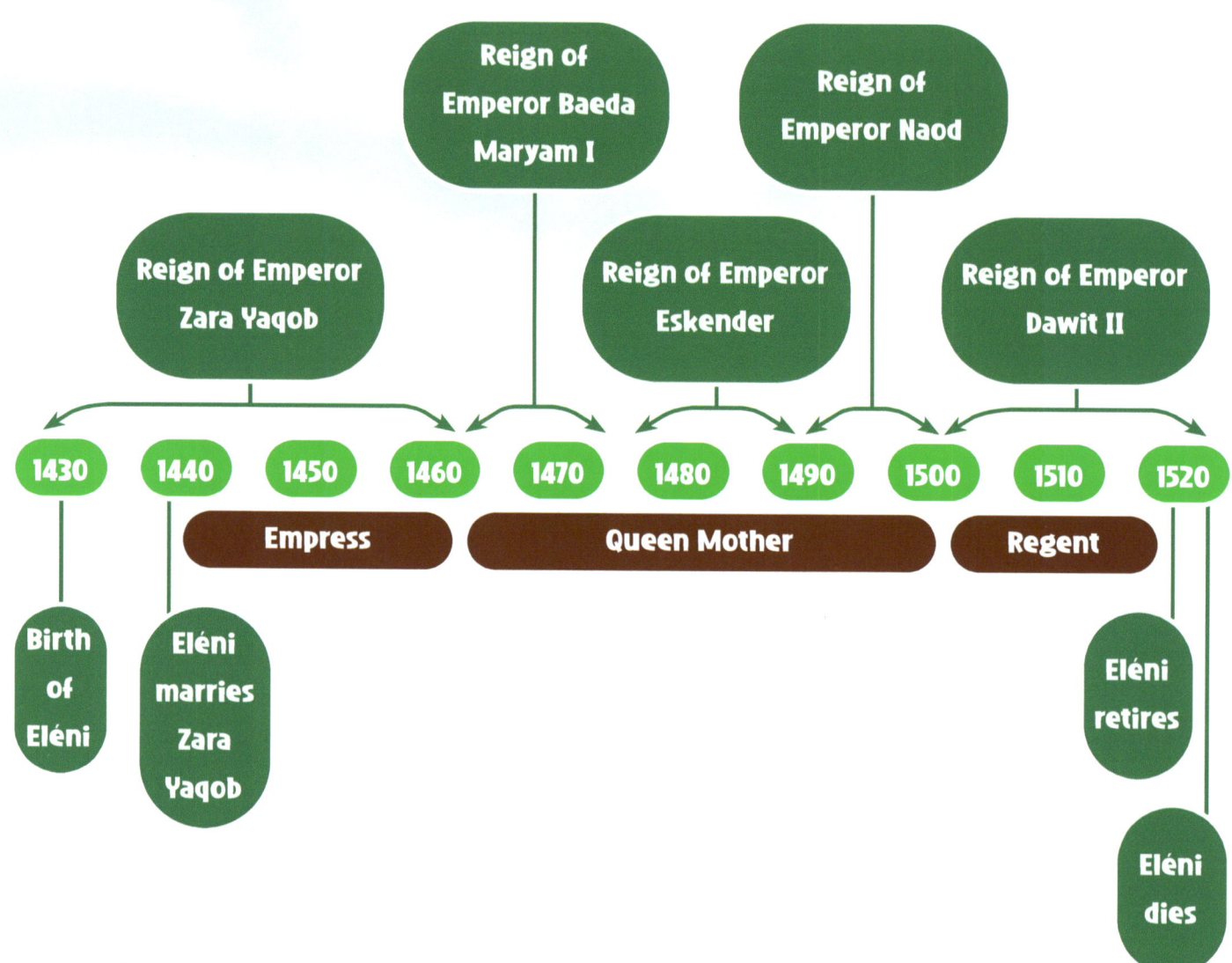

Family Tree

References

Bayu, Yeshambel K. "Empress Eléni: Overturning Falsified Narratives on Her Consort, Ethnicity, and Religious Background." *The Ethiopian Journal of Social Sciences*, vol. 8, no. 1, May 2022, pp. 1-27. https://www.ajol.info/index.php/ejss/article/view/241085.

Garkebo, Tadesse Sibamo. *Documentation and Description of Hadiyya*. 2015. Addis Ababa University, PhD. dissertation.

Pankhurst, Rita. "Taytu's Foremothers, Queen Eléni, Queen Sabla Wangel and Bati Del Wamara." *Proceedings of the 16th International Conference of Ethiopian Studies, Trondheim, 2009*. Edited by Svein Ege, Harald Aspen, Birhanu Teferra and Shiferaw Bekele, 2009, pp. 51-63.

Owens, Travis. *Beleaguered Muslim Fortresses and Ethiopian Imperial Expansion from the 13th to the 16th Century*. 2008. Naval Postgraduate School, Master's thesis.

Selassie, Tsehai Berhane. "Ba'eda Maryam." *Encyclopedia Africana Dictionary of African Biography, Volume 1, Ethiopia – Ghana,* edited by L.H. Ofosu-Appiah, Reference Publications Inc., 1977, p. 54.

Aragay, Merid Wolde. "Eléni." *Encyclopedia Africana Dictionary of African Biography, Volume 1, Ethiopia – Ghana,* edited by L.H. Ofosu-Appiah, Reference Publications Inc., 1977, p. 63.

Selassie, Tsehai Berhane. "Zare'a Ya'eqob." *Encyclopedia Africana Dictionary of African Biography, Volume 1, Ethiopia – Ghana,* edited by L.H. Ofosu-Appiah, Reference Publications Inc., 1977, pp. 155-156.

Hassen, Mohammed. *The Oromo of Ethiopia, 1500-1850: With Special Emphasis on the Gibe Region.* 1983. University of London, PhD dissertation.

Fun Fact About Ethiopia

Ethiopia is home to the lowest geographic location in Africa, the Danakil Depression. It is a small place close to Ethiopia's border with Eritrea. This is a plain about 124 miles from north to south, and 31 miles wide, and sits at 410 feet below sea level. It's very hot with an average daily temperature of 93.92 degrees Fahrenheit; however, some days the temperature may exceed 122 degrees Fahrenheit. It is the location of about twenty-five percent of Africa's volcanoes. It has salt flats and hot springs. Salt flats are areas where salt and other minerals, such as sulfur, cover the ground.

Other Books in the Heritage Collection

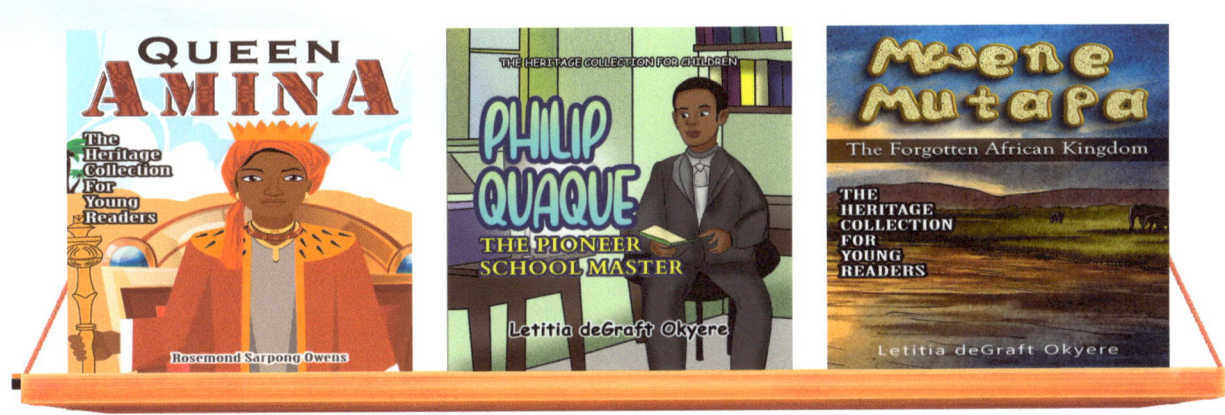
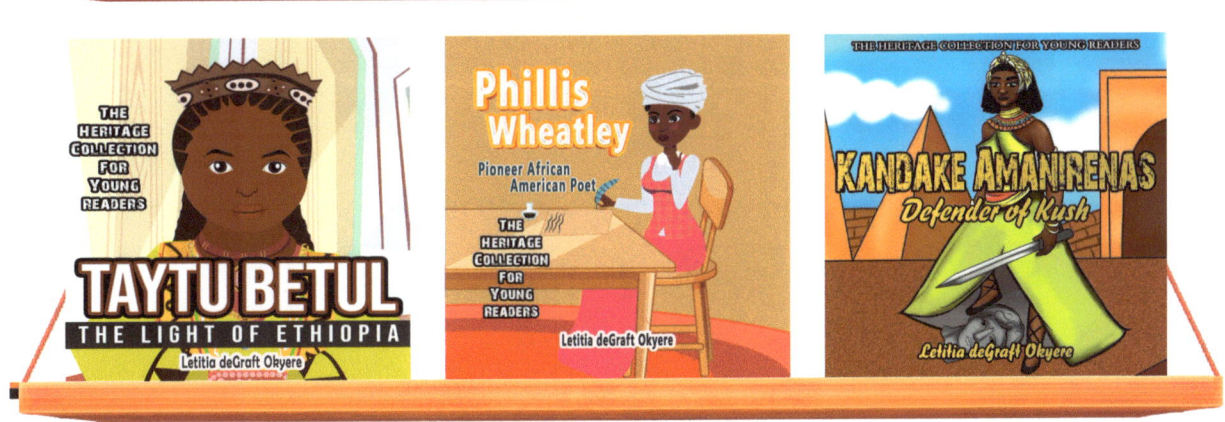

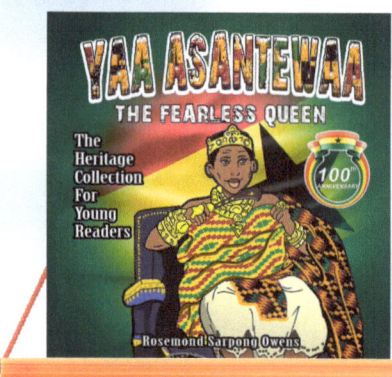
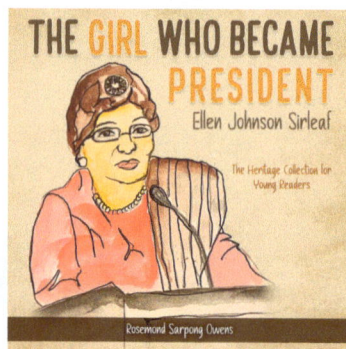
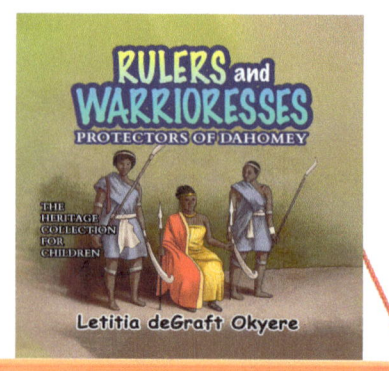
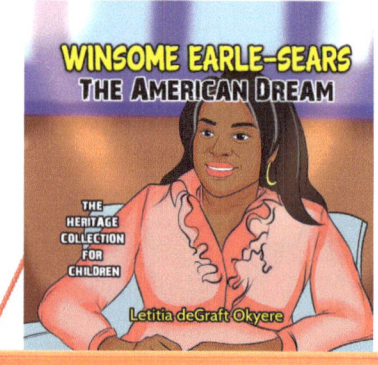
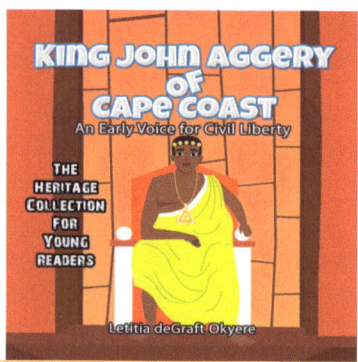

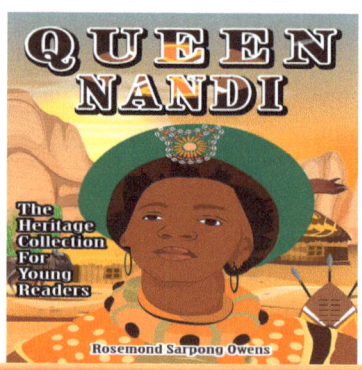
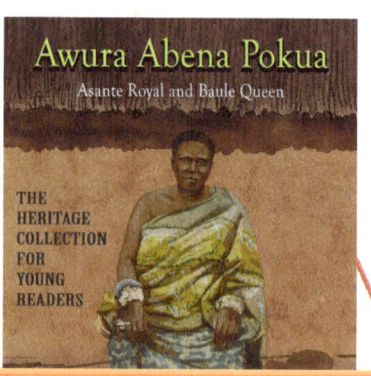

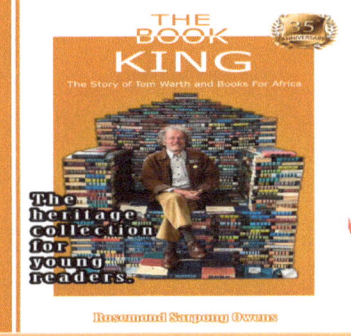
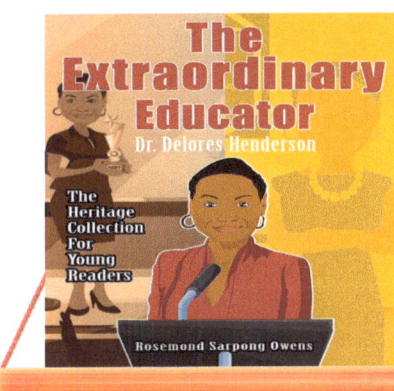
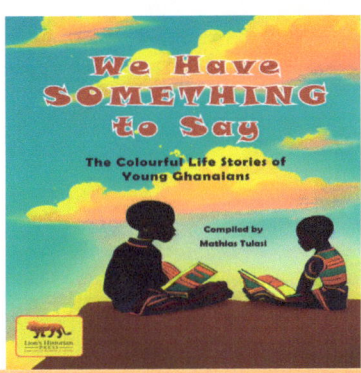
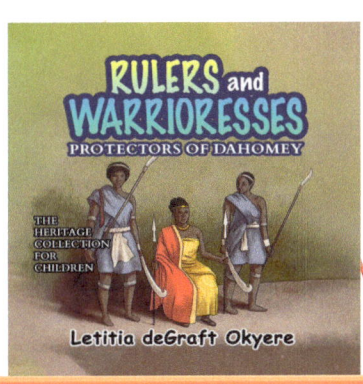

Author's Note

Through the Heritage Collection's historical biographies for children, the author endeavors to tell the stories of men and women of African descent who changed the course of events within their circles of influence.

Historical biographies are important for child development. When a child can see him- or herself represented in the life of people who grew up to effect social, economic, or political change, he or she is more likely to be inspired to meet and overcome life's challenges.

Thus, the author's purpose is simple: to enable children to fulfill their destinies by seeing themselves through others who rose above difficulties to bring about change.

www.ingramcontent.com/pod-product-compliance
Lightning Source LLC
Chambersburg PA
CBHW041406010526
44107CB00015B/1095